W9-AET-714

Cool STEAM Careers

Cyber Cop

Wil Mara

Published in the United States of America by Cherry Lake Publishing
Ann Arbor, Michigan
www.cherrylakepublishing.com

Content Adviser: law enforcement members
Reading Adviser: Marla Conn, ReadAbility, Inc.

Photo Credits: © AndreyPopov/Thinkstock.com, cover, 1, 17; © CREATISTA/Shutterstock Images, 5; © Comstock
Images/Thinkstock.com, 6; © Steve Hix/Fuze/Thinkstock.com, 7; © AnaBGD/Thinkstock.com, 8; © Paula Solloway/
Alamy, 11; © Burlingham/Shutterstock Images, 12; © Macrovector/Shutterstock Images, 15; © VGstockstudio/
Shutterstock Images, 16; © moodboard/Thinkstock.com, 18, 21, 29; © PeopleImages/istockphoto.com, 22; © JMiks/
Shutterstock Images, 25; © RosaIreneBetancourt 8/Alamy, 26

Copyright ©2016 by Cherry Lake Publishing
All rights reserved. No part of this book may be reproduced or utilized in
any form or by any means without written permission from the publisher.

Library of Congress Cataloging-in-Publication Data

Mara, Wil.
  Cyber cop/Wil Mara.
    pages cm.—(Cool STEAM careers)
  Includes index.
  ISBN 978-1-63362-557-0 (hardcover)—ISBN 978-1-63362-737-6 (pdf)—ISBN 978-1-63362-647-8 (pbk.)—
ISBN 978-1-63362-827-4 (ebook)
  1. Computer crimes—Investigation—Juvenile literature. 2. Police—Juvenile literature. 3. Criminal investigation—
Juvenile literature. I. Title.

HV8079.C65M27 2016
363.25'968—dc23
                              2015005358

Cherry Lake Publishing would like to acknowledge the work of
the Partnership for 21st Century Skills. Please visit *www.p21.org*
for more information.

Printed in the United States of America
Corporate Graphics

ABOUT THE AUTHOR

Wil Mara is an award-winning, best-selling author of more than 150 books, many of which are
educational titles for young readers. Further information about his work can be found at
www.wilmara.com.

TABLE OF CONTENTS

STEAM is the acronym for Science, Technology, Engineering, Arts, and Mathematics. In this book, you will read about how each of these study areas is connected to a career in cyber law enforcement.

CHAPTER 1

CRIME TIME

Computers are wonderful, aren't they? You can buy things online and never have to step out of your house. You can write reports for school and make a hundred typing mistakes—and then correct them. And you can communicate with people on the other side of the world in real time.

Unfortunately, the awesome freedom that all this new technology provides has a downside. Anyone who wants to use it dishonestly can plug in and power up just as easily as you can. Let's consider a few examples.

Your smartphone may have a security flaw that you aren't aware of.

Ten-year-old Jenna just got a cool new iPhone app. Excited to start using the app just like her friends, she downloads it, connects to the Internet, and has a great time playing the game with everybody. Meanwhile, what she and her online pals don't know is that the app is actually sending copies of their contact lists to someone sitting on the other side of the world.

Twenty-eight-year-old Jacob just spent the last year of his life writing a movie script. His dreams come true when a major studio offers him a contract and says it's

Many people use computers every day, but technology always comes with risks.

going to be made into a feature film starring Will Ferrell. Wanting it to be perfect, Jacob decides to do a little more work on it before sending it to the studio. But then his computer gets hit by a **virus**. All of his data is wiped out—including the script that he spent so much time and effort putting together.

Forty-nine-year-old Robbie is a veteran rock star who hasn't released a new CD in a while. But he just spent the last ten months in the studio putting together what is rumored to be the greatest album of

Buying songs legally is a better way to support musicians than downloading them from other sources.

his career. He's poured his heart and soul into it, and he believes it'll bring him back to superstardom. When it hits the stores, both the public and the critics go crazy over it. But within one week, it has been copied down to MP3 files and offered for free on thousands of illegal Web sites.

Businesses are also at risk for **cyber** crimes. In 2014, Sony Pictures Entertainment faced a huge challenge. A group who called themselves the Guardians of Peace hacked into Sony's system, froze all of their computers,

Getting hit with a cyber crime can feel pretty scary.

and sent threatening messages. The group stole brand-new movies and put them online before they were in the theaters. They published e-mails that had personal information about employees and actors. As of 2015, Sony was still experiencing problems from the hack.

It's time to call in the cyber cops! Who is responsible when information that is **confidential** or under **copyright** is taken or destroyed? Does the Web site or app from which the information was stolen owe something to the victims? Are the victims themselves responsible in any way? Debate on this issue becomes more critical as computer crimes become more sophisticated.

THINK ABOUT TECHNOLOGY

Technology saves us time and provides us with entertainment and convenience, but criminals also have access to technology. Happily, there are numerous Web sites that offer useful information on what you can do to protect yourself. Never, ever give anyone online your personal information such as your full name, address, or date of birth.

CHAPTER 2

WHO ARE CYBER COPS?

These examples all describe actual cyber crimes. These are illegal acts committed using computer technology. Cyber cops work to stamp out this type of crime. Their efforts help crime victims like those in the stories. Cyber cops also educate the public about preventing these crimes.

Cyber cops can be members of city, county, or state police departments. They may be part of special squads within national organizations like the United States Postal Service or the Bureau of Alcohol, Tobacco,

Firearms and Explosives (ATF). They may be part of the Secret Service or the Federal Bureau of Investigation (FBI). Cyber cops may also work for private companies or volunteer their services in citizens' groups formed to help fight computer crime.

Cyber cops usually do not look for smashed windows, broken locks, and other such clues. Instead, they comb

Some cyber cops offer classes on how to use computers safely.

Cyber cops use their strong knowledge of computers to search for clues.

[21ST CENTURY SKILLS LIBRARY]

through computer files to see where and how the thieves got in. They search for weaknesses in the computer programs the victim is using. In addition, they look for cyber fingerprints—clues left behind in the computer programs that have been broken into. Through these clues, cyber cops are often able to catch the criminals and strengthen the security systems.

THINK ABOUT MATH

A cyber cop must have the ability to organize information. Arranging actions in a certain order or pattern according to specific rules is a component of mathematics. Math classes give students an understanding of patterns of numbers, letters, words, pictures, and mathematical operations.

CHAPTER 3

ON THE JOB

Cyber detectives explained to Jenna's parents that she was the victim of **malware**. Malware is spread by criminals who design programs that look appealing and are usually given away for free, making them all the more tempting. Once the app has been downloaded, it begins digging through a person's computer or smartphone, looking for sensitive information. It then sends that information back to the criminals. Cyber cops advised Jenna not to download any more programs without informing her parents first. Her parents could go on the

Some games seem innocent, but they can cause damage to your computer or smartphone.

Internet first and see if those programs perform **malicious** functions and if warnings about them have been posted.

The screenwriter losing his movie script had his computer hit by a virus. In this instance, the criminals were simply trying to be pests. In some cases, cyber cops can trace the virus back to its creator. But some cyber criminals know how to cover their tracks with the aid of advanced technology.

In the case of the rock star having his new album given away for free, this is an example of copyright violation.

Some people film movies in theaters and then post them online, which is illegal.

Thousands of musicians have had their hard work stolen and then handed out, without any profit going back into their pockets. Often, the criminals involved are located in different countries, where laws to protect against this type of threat have not yet been written. That means cyber cops have almost no power to stop them. This crime is often called **pirating**.

Many computer **hackers** think that breaking into a security system is a sign of how smart they are. However, they are criminals like any other. Cyber cops have solved thousands of cases in recent years. In one case, criminals were selling fake credit cards and personal information. The stolen information was used to withdraw money or buy things using the name of the person whose identity had been stolen. Other criminals set up a Web site called Silk Road, a secret marketplace for illegal goods. Cyber cops from the FBI and other U.S. agencies worked with authorities in Europe to catch them.

Cyber cops track down criminals who steal credit card information and commit other cyber crimes.

Even though the crimes take place online, the people who commit them can get arrested in real life.

18

Sometimes, people who have never been in trouble before still think they can get away with computer crimes. In 2014, a student at Purdue University was taking a somewhat relaxed approach to his coursework. He was slacking on his homework, so, predictably enough, he was failing every class. No problem, though—he simply hacked into his professors' databases and changed all his grades! Unfortunately for him, he got caught by cyber cops. Not only was he booted from the school, but he also had to spend three months in jail. That crime will likely be on his record when he applies for jobs in the future.

THINK ABOUT SCIENCE

Cyber cops need to have strong academic backgrounds. More importantly, they need to keep learning. If a career as a cyber cop sounds interesting to you, try getting involved in clubs or camps that involve circuit boards, processors, chips, electronic equipment, and computer hardware and software, including applications and programming.

TRAINING

How do you fight an enemy you can't see and whose weapon—the computer—is everywhere? This is where cyber cop training comes in. This training covers many academic subjects, including economics, psychology, and foreign languages.

A degree in computer science provides a fine basis for becoming a cyber cop. College training in economics and languages other than English would help a cyber cop solve banking crimes that start outside the United States. Studying international law and international relations also is helpful.

People studying to be cyber cops need to be extremely skilled on computers.

Courses in criminal justice are necessary, especially those that relate to computer crimes. Cyber cops must make sure they are ready for each new generation of "bad guys." Future cyber cops often spend time learning programming and other computer-related skills.

Cyber cops follow the trails of the criminals throughout the physical world, too. Recently, FBI cyber cops traveled to Turkey and Morocco to share information with officials about cyber criminals operating there. This kind of cooperation can be essential to cracking a case.

Cyber cops work together to figure out the best ways to catch criminals.

Istanbul sits on both sides of a narrow waterway that separates Europe and the Middle East. Its location makes it an ideal place for cyber cops monitoring illegal activities in both areas.

The FBI needs agents who speak other languages and have highly developed computer skills. A person with these two qualifications would be considered an ideal candidate for the FBI. These people must also meet the FBI's general hiring requirements. Then they would very likely be given top priority in hiring and job choice.

THINK ABOUT ART

*Good communication skills are important when a cyber cop testifies in court. He or she must talk to the jury in such a way that technical information is made clear to them. A little acting skill can't hurt either. At times the cyber cop travels through the online world as an actor. Success leads to catching potential kidnappers, **stalkers**, and other types of criminals.*

CHAPTER 5

THE FUTURE

As computers become more advanced, so do cyber crimes. It's a vicious cycle—the crooks get better at committing crimes, and the cyber cops learn to catch them. Then newer and better technologies come out, the crooks master them, and the whole process starts again.

What's unsettling is how clever the criminals are becoming. In 2013, a man in Great Britain, with help from two associates in Australia and Sweden, managed to hack into the military defense systems of the United States. This poses a high risk to national security.

There is another new form of hacking is known as **ransomware**—programs that essentially hold your critical data hostage until you pay some form of ransom. It can be transmitted to your computer through something as simple as an e-mail with an inviting subject line like "Get an Apple iPad for FREE!" or

Some viruses can do a lot of damage, but others are just annoying.

The Department of Defense wants to hire people who have strong technology skills.

"Your Best Friend Just Sent You a Really Funny Picture." Once that e-mail is opened, the ransomware automatically downloads and installs itself. Links like these are also common in social media posts, and are threats to both computers and smartphones. Don't ever click on them!

Many crime-fighting organizations have formed special teams of cyber cops. One of these types of teams is the FBI Cyber Action Teams, or CAT. A CAT fights

THINK ABOUT ENGINEERING

According to the University of Michigan, computer engineering majors have careers anywhere there are computers, which is virtually everywhere. While a degree is not required to be a part of an FBI CAT, a responsibility of the job is to maintain awareness of potential cyber-attack technologies, methods, and signatures. Taking courses in computer architecture, computer systems, and software development would be valuable for a career as a cyber cop.

both present and future cyber crime. Each team is made up of FBI agents and specialists in computer crime. A team is ready to travel to the scene at a moment's notice. CATs carry hardware and software that allow them to set up a field office for up to six months anywhere in the world. In fact, it was a CAT, together with local authorities, that ran the successful operations in Turkey and Morocco.

Being a cyber cop isn't just an exciting job. It's going to be one of the most critical and in-demand professions in the years ahead. Computers will probably always be around, and that means (unfortunately) that cyber criminals will be around as well. If you're truly interested in making the world a safer place and have a knack for technology, this is one job you may want to seriously consider.

Always be careful what personal information you put online, and what files you choose to download.

THINK ABOUT IT

The word *cyber* is used often. Go online or visit the library to determine when the word was first used. What are the word's origins? How many words can you think of that start with "cyber-"?

Go online to look up some Internet safety tips. How can you protect your laptop and smartphone from cyber crimes? Which of these safety tips are you already following? What things should you start doing?

Technology is changing rapidly. The ways people commit computer crimes are changing, and the ways cyber cops track them are also changing. What inventions do you think would be helpful for law enforcement to have in the future?

LEARN MORE

FURTHER READING

Cindrich, Sharon. *A Smart Girl's Guide to the Internet*. Middleton, Wisconsin: American Girl (Quality), 2009.

Loh-Hagan, Virginia. *Ethical Hacker*. Ann Arbor, Michigan: Cherry Lake Publishing, 2016.

Mitra, Ananda. *Digital Security: Cyber Terror and Cyber Security*. New York: Chelsea House, 2010.

WEB SITE

The FBI: Kids—Safety Tips
www.fbi.gov/kids/k5th/safety2.htm
This site offers tips on how you can stay safe on the Internet.

McGruff the Crime Dog
www.mcgruff.org/#/Main
Check out fun games, videos, and computer safety advice with McGruff the Crime Dog.

Today's Parent: 30 Fun and Safe Kids' Websites
http://www.todaysparent.com/kids/technology/30-fun-and-safe-kids-websites
Next time you want to play an online game, try visiting one from this list.

GLOSSARY

confidential (kahn-fi-DEN-shuhl) secret

copyright (KAH-pee-rite) the legal right to control the use of something created, such as a song or book

cyber (SYE-bur) having to do with computer networks

hackers (HAK-erz) people who break into important, often secret, computer files, sometimes just to see if the break-in can be accomplished

malicious (muh-LISH-uhs) intended to hurt or embarrass someone

malware (MAL-wair) software that draws sensitive information from your computer and then sends it back to the criminals using it

pirating (PYE-rit-ing) making unauthorized copies of music, film, a computer game, or other entertainment created by someone else and selling them illegally

ransomware (RAN-suhm-wair) software that locks up or steals sensitive information from your computer with the intent of being given back to you only after you pay for it in some way

stalkers (STAWK-erz) people who hunt or track other people in a quiet, secret way

virus (VYE-ruhs) a computer program, hidden within another, seemingly innocent program, that produces many copies of itself and is designed to destroy a computer system or damage data

INDEX

J 363.25 MARA

Mara, Wil.
Cyber cop

SOF

R4002334992

SOUTH FULTON BRANCH
Atlanta-Fulton Public Library